TREE VIPERS

THE SNAKE DISCOVERY LIBRARY

Sherie Bargar   Linda Johnson

Photographer/Consultant: George Van Horn

Rourke Enterprises, Inc.
Vero Beach, Florida 32964

Library of Congress Cataloging in Publication Data

Bargar, Sherie, 1944-
    Tree vipers.

    (The Snake discovery library)
    Includes index.
    Summary: Discusses that viper which spends its
life in the trees of tropical forests.
    1. Viperidae—Juvenile literature.   2. Pit-vipers—
Juvenile literature.   3. Snakes—Juvenile literature.
[1. Snakes]   I. Johnson, Linda, 1947-   . II. Van Horn,
George, ill.   III. Title.   IV. Series: Bargar, Sherie,
1944-   .   Snake discovery library.
QL666.069B396   1987   597.96   87-12793
ISBN 0-86592-245-4

Title Photo:
Purple Spotted Pit Viper
Trimeresrus purpureomaculatus

TABLE OF CONTENTS

TREE VIPERS

All species of tree vipers are members of the *Crotalidae* or *Viperidae* families. Adaptation to tree life has created changes in both their behavior and their body structure. **Agile** muscular bodies and prehensile tails are features that are essential for life in the trees. Prehensile tails are ones which have changed over the years to enable tree vipers to hold on to branches. Moving from limb to limb in trees is possible because their muscular bodies support them as their prehensile tails ease them across open spaces. Their unique body features make these tree dwelling snakes a rare visitor on the forest floor.

Yellow Eyelash Viper
Bothrops schelegeli

WHERE THEY LIVE

The dense tropical forests of Asia, Africa, Central, and South America are the common habitats of the tree viper. Tropical forests have heavy **precipitation** and **condensation** which collect on tree leaves. Tree vipers drink the moisture from the leaves. This moisture is their primary source of drinking water. While some species prefer the **canopy** of the tropical forests, others may live just a few feet off the ground.

Eyelash Viper Habitat

HOW THEY LOOK

A large distinct head marks the beginning of the tree viper's muscular body which may be between 2 and 5 feet long. The keeled scales which have a ridge down the middle are sometimes leaf-like in appearance. This **camouflages** the snake in the trees. Green, black, orange, yellow, red, blue, brown, purple, and combinations of these colors appear in unlimited patterns and color combinations on tree vipers.

Pink Eyelash Viper
Bothrops schelegeli

THEIR SENSES

    Beneath the **canopy** of the dimly lit tropical forest, the tree viper's large eyes search for **prey**. Branch movement and vibrations warn the snake of approaching **prey**. The tongue and Jacobson's organ identify the source of motion at close range. The tongue flicks out and brings scent particles back to be **analyzed** by the Jacobson's organ in the roof of the mouth. Within seconds the snake identifies the **intruder** and takes the appropriate action.

High Mountain Tree Viper
Bothrops nigroviridis

African Bush Viper
Atheris squamigera robusta

A group of African Bush Vipers
Bothrops nigroviridis

THE HEAD AND MOUTH

Tree vipers in the *Crotalidae* family have heat receptor pits while those in the *Viperidae* family do not. Large **venom** glands are located behind the eyes on their distinct heads. Fangs are folded against the roof of the mouth when not being used. During a bite the fangs are extended. **Venom** glands are voluntarily **contracted** to force strong **venom** through long hollow fangs and into the **prey**. The jaws stretch like a rubber band to swallow the animal whole. The windpipe extends from the throat to the front of the mouth and allows the snake to breathe while swallowing **prey**.

14

Eyelash Viper in Defense Posture
Bothrops schelegeli

Nostril

Heat receptor pit

Fangs in sheaths

Windpipe

BABY TREE VIPERS

A female tree viper may give birth twice a year. Baby tree vipers are hatched from egg membranes during the rainy season. Egg membranes are thin and rubbery shells which surround the unborn snake. The young snake slits the egg membrane with its **egg tooth** at the moment of birth. As the babies are born, they actively grasp for the security of a branch. At birth the young tree vipers weigh under a quarter of an ounce and are about 6 inches long. Often their coloring is different from the adult. The baby tree vipers take care of themselves from birth.

South American Palm Viper
Bothrops bilineatus

PREY

Hidden from view, the tree viper relies on surprise as the key to successful hunting. Frogs, lizards, birds, and small mammals are its usual **prey**. The tree viper injects its **venom**. Without releasing its catch, the tree viper awaits the death of its **prey** and then swallows it whole. To release the grip before swallowing might result in dropping the prey to the ground and losing the meal.

Eyelash Viper feeding on a mouse
Bothrops schelegeli

THEIR DEFENSE

Camouflaged by its color and patterns, the tree viper may remain unseen by an enemy. **Camouflage** is the most important element of its defense. When approached by an enemy, the tree viper stands its ground by extending and shaking its tail to scare the enemy. If the enemy continues to move closer, some tree vipers strike. Other species leap off of their tree branches to drop out of sight in the dense tropical forest.

Asian Bamboo Viper
Trimeresurus stejnegeri

TREE VIPERS AND PEOPLE

Tree vipers are feared throughout the world. Many people, unaware of the **camouflaged** tree viper, are bitten on the face and head as they venture through the tropical forest. During the Vietnam War, tree vipers were used as booby traps in guerilla warfare. Enemy soldiers tied 3 or 4 tree vipers together by their tails with leather thongs. The angry snakes were hung by their tails to bite unsuspecting soldiers in the face as they walked through the forest.

GLOSSARY

agile (AG ile) — Easy and quick moving.

analyze (AN a lyze) analyzed — To find out what something is.

camouflage (CAM ou flage) camouflaged, camouflages — The color of an animal's skin that matches the ground around it.

canopy (CAN o py) — The top layer of the trees covering the forest.

condensation (con den SA tion) — Vapor turned to liquid.

contract (CON tract) contracted — Squeeze.

egg tooth (EGG TOOTH) — A temporary tiny ridge which is very sharp and used to open the egg. It is on the top of a baby snake's nose.

intruder (in TRUD er) — One who approaches another and is not welcome.

precipitation (pre cip i TA tion) — Rain.

prey (PREY) — An animal hunted or killed by another animal for food.

venom (VEN om) — A chemical made in animals that makes other animals and people sick or kills them.

INDEX